40 DAY NEW COVENANT DEVOTIONAL

BISI OLADIPUPO

SPRINGS OF LIFE PUBLISHING

Copyright © 2023 by Bisi Oladipupo

Springs of life publishing

ISBN: 978-1-915269-28-7 (ePub e-book)

ISBN: (978-1-915269-27-0 paperback)

All Rights Reserved.

No part of this book may be used or reproduced by any means, graphic, electronic, or mechanical, including photocopying, recording, taping, or by any information storage retrieval system without the written permission of the publisher except in the case of brief quotations embodied in critical articles and reviews.

Printed in the United Kingdom

Unless otherwise indicated, scripture quotations are taken from the New King James Version.

Scripture taken from the New King James Version®. Copyright © 1982 by Thomas Nelson. Used by permission. All rights reserved.

Scripture quotations from The Authorized (King James) Version. Rights in the Authorized Version in the United Kingdom are vested in the Crown. Reproduced by permission of the Crown's patentee, Cambridge University Press.

Scripture quotations marked (AMP) are taken from the Amplified Bible, Copyright © 2015 by The Lockman Foundation. Used by permission.

CONTENTS

Dedication	VI
Introduction	VII
1. Day 1: We Are Now Sons of God	1
2. Day 2: Joint Heirs With Christ	3
3. Day 3: Liberty is Ours	5
4. Day 4: This Cup Is the New Testament in My Blood	7
5. Day 5: He is our God and we are His people	9
6. Day 6: Accepted In the Beloved	11
7. Day 7: Part of a New Kingdom	13
8. Day 8: A Chosen Generation and Royal Priesthood	15
9. Day 9: Risen with Christ	17
10. Day 10: Intimacy with God	19
11. Day 11: The Inner Witness	21

12. Day 12: We Are Healed — 22
13. Day 13: We have obtained the Mercy of God — 23
14. Day 14: Access to the Mercy of God — 25
15. Day 15: Access to the Grace of God — 27
16. Day 16: We Have Been Given the Ministry of Reconciliation — 29
17. Day 17: We Are the Righteousness of God in Christ — 31
18. Day 18: Jesus Christ is Our High Priest — 33
19. Day 19: A New Creation in Christ Jesus — 35
20. Day 20: Dead to Sin — 37
21. Day 21: Ability to Bear Fruit of the Spirit — 39
22. Day 22: We Can Call God Our Father — 40
23. Day 23: Justified By Faith — 42
24. Day 24: Forgiveness of Sins — 43
25. Day 25: Peace with God — 45
26. Day 26: God's Love Has Been Poured into our Hearts — 46
27. Day 27: We Can Be Led by the Spirit of God — 48
28. Day 28: Living Through Christ Jesus — 50
29. Day 29: Seated With Christ in Heavenly Places — 52
30. Day 30: Authority to Use the Name of Jesus — 53
31. Day 31: The Promise of the Holy Spirit — 55
32. Day 32: The Gifts of the Holy Spirit Can Work Through Us — 57

33.	Day 33: Prosperity	59
34.	Day 34: Christ Now Lives in Us	61
35.	Day 35: Boldness to Come unto the Throne of Grace	63
36.	Day 36: We are the Temple of the Living God	65
37.	Day 37: The Kingdom of God is Within You	67
38.	Day 38: Demonstration of the Power of God	69
39.	Day 39: Ability to Pray in the Holy Spirit	71
40.	Day 40: Ability to Live for Christ	73
Salvation Prayer		75
Also By Bisi		76
About Author		78
Afterword		79

To Jesus Christ my Lord and saviour; to Him alone that laid down His life that l might have life eternal. To Him that lead captivity captive and gave gifts unto men (Ephesians 4; 8). One of those gifts is writing!

Bisi Oladipupo

Introduction

Why a devotional?

As believers, we need to know what belongs to us under our better covenant (Hebrews 8:6).

Our God is a covenant-keeping God. We only need to see how far our God went to deliver the children of Israel out of Egypt. It was simply because of His covenant (Deuteronomy 7:8).

I recommend you get a copy of the book, *A Better Covenant,* by Bisi Oladipupo. In the book, I discussed the importance of a covenant, how we can benefit from it, and much more.

This devotional is simply to reinforce what we have under our New Covenant in a devotional form. This will give us gradual daily bites on what belongs to us, and as we meditate on these, they will become part of our practical experience while walking in revelation knowledge.

BISI OLADIPUPO

Enjoy and be blessed!

DAY 1: WE ARE NOW SONS OF GOD

"*He came to His [c]own, and His [d]own did not receive Him. 12 But as many as received Him, to them He gave the [e]right to become children of God, to those who believe in His name:*" (John 1:11-12)

To what extent will a good earthly father be there for his own son? Did you know that we are sons of God under the New Covenant? Have you ever heard of a child bragging about their father on the playground?

According to Scripture, we are children of God. We know that our Heavenly Father is good. What child in the natural world would hesitate to run to their father at all times?

The Bible says, "Now are we the sons of God" (1 John 3:2; KJV). Every son would want to represent their father well.

"Therefore be imitators of God as dear children. ² And walk in love, as Christ also has loved us and given Himself for us, an offering and a sacrifice to God for a sweet-smelling aroma" (Ephesians 5:1-2).

As we go about our day, let us walk as sons of God and truly represent our Heavenly Father.

Prayer: Lord, help me to see myself the way you see me. Help me to truly represent you today in word and deed, in Jesus' name.

Day 2: Joint Heirs With Christ

"*The Spirit Himself bears witness with our spirit that we are children of God, *17* and if children, then heirs—heirs of God and joint heirs with Christ, if indeed we suffer with Him, that we may also be glorified together*" (Romans 8:16-17).

Not only are we children of God, but we are also heirs of God and joint heirs with Christ. What does that look like?

Christ paid the price and has been rewarded by the Father (Revelation 3:21). We also have our part to play in this kingdom. If you notice the above phrase, it says, "*if indeed we suffer with Him, that we may also be glorified together*".

When we know that we are joint heirs with Christ, we will be prepared to do what it takes to finish our race well. Our God is a great rewarder.

"To him who overcomes I will grant to sit with Me on My throne, as I also overcame and sat down with My Father on His throne" (Revelation 3:21).

Prayer: Lord, help me get a proper perspective on things above and help me finish my race well in Jesus' name.

Day 3: Liberty is Ours

"Behold, there was a woman which had a spirit of infirmity eighteen years, and was bowed together, and could in no wise lift up herself. ¹² And when Jesus saw her, he called her to him, and said unto her, Woman, thou art loosed from thine infirmity. ¹³ And he laid his hands on her: and immediately she was made straight, and glorified God. *¹⁶ And ought not this woman, being a daughter of Abraham, whom Satan hath bound, lo, these eighteen years, be loosed from this bond on the sabbath day?"* (Luke 13:11-13, 16; KJV).

If the daughter of Abraham ought not to be bound by a spirit of infirmity, neither should the seed of Abraham be bound either. In Christ Jesus, we are Abraham's seed (Galatians 3:29).

We must stand our ground on what belongs to us through Christ Jesus, including liberty. The Lord did not want this woman bound, and neither does He want us bound by any form of infirmity.

BISI OLADIPUPO

Prayer: I take my authority in Christ Jesus, and I resist any form of infirmity in Jesus' name.

Day 4: This Cup Is the New Testament in My Blood

"In the same manner He also took the cup after supper, saying, "This cup is the new covenant in My blood. This do, as often as you drink it, in remembrance of Me" (1 Corinthians 11:25).

Taking the Lord's Supper is an ordinance that reminds us of our New Covenant.

The cup is the suffering of the Lord (Matthew 26:39), the price Jesus Christ, our Lord, paid in His blood for our New Covenant.

So, when we come to the Lord's table, it is an opportunity and a reminder that Jesus used His blood to pay for our covenant.

Therefore, as we come to the Lord's table, remember all Christ has done for us and enforce our benefits under the New Covenant.

Prayer: Father, I thank you for the price that Jesus Christ paid for our New Covenant. Lord, help me by your grace to be diligent in learning and understanding what belongs to me and to make this a practical reality in every area of my life, in Jesus' name.

DAY 5: HE IS OUR GOD AND WE ARE HIS PEOPLE

"*For this is the covenant that I will make with the house of Israel after those days, says the Lord: I will put My laws in their mind and write them on their hearts; and I will be their God, and they shall be My people*" (Hebrews 8:10).

God is committed to us under this covenant: He will be a God to us, and we shall be His people.

That really needs to sink in.

So, why do we worry and run around instead of running to God in times of need? We must be confident under this covenant that God has our back. This is simply amazing, and we are His people. Therefore, we do belong to God.

The one who sits upon the throne is our God (Revelation 5:13).

So, do you have any cares today? Why not cast them upon Him? Look at the Old Testament and see how God fought for His people. He is our God.

Prayer: Father, I thank you that you are my God, and I belong to you.

DAY 6: ACCEPTED IN THE BELOVED

"*Having predestined us to adoption as sons by Jesus Christ to Himself, according to the good pleasure of His will, ⁶ to the praise of the glory of His grace, by which He [a]made us accepted in the Beloved* (Ephesians 1:5-6).

We have been accepted by Jesus Christ. God, our Father, has opened His arms wide to receive us in Christ Jesus.

When we come to God the Father, the Lord sees us in His beloved Son, Jesus Christ. Did you know that the same love the Father has for Jesus Christ is bestowed on us (John 17:23)?

That is very powerful. We also are beloved of God (1 John 3:2).

We need to meditate on this reality and accept the love of God. This will really have a positive impact on our walk with the Lord.

Confession: Father, I thank you that I am accepted in the family of the beloved, and you love me as you love Jesus Christ.

Day 7: Part of a New Kingdom

"*Who hath delivered us from the power of darkness, and hath translated us into the kingdom of his dear Son:*" (Colossians 1:13; KJV)

Under the New Covenant, those who have made Jesus Christ their Lord and Saviour are in a different kingdom.

If a person moved from one nation to another, they would have to abide by the rules of the nation they moved into. They would also need to know how things operate in that new territory.

We now belong to the kingdom of our Lord and Saviour, Jesus Christ. What a privilege and an honour! Now, we need to know how things operate in this new kingdom and what belongs to us.

Prayer: Father, thank you for all that Jesus Christ has done for me. Father, I pray that you open the eyes of my understanding so I know what belongs to me in this new kingdom in Jesus' name.

Day 8: A Chosen Generation and Royal Priesthood

*"**B**ut you are a chosen generation, a royal priesthood, a holy nation, His own special people, that you may proclaim the praises of Him who called you out of darkness into His marvelous light;"* (1 Peter 2:9).

We are not of this world (John 17:16). We are chosen by God and a royal priesthood. The children of Israel in the Old Covenant had a similar position with God (Exodus 19:5-6).

So, what does a priest do? A priest represents God, prays for others, and offers sacrifices to God, among other things. According to scripture, we are all in ministry. We are all priests, and not just any priest, but royal priests. Jesus Christ has made us priests unto God (Revelation

1:6). Under the New Covenant, our sacrifices are different (1 Peter 2:5).

As we go about our day, let us remember that we represent God. Let us pray and share the gospel of good news with others.

Prayer: Thank you, Father, that Jesus Christ has made me a priest unto you. Give me an understanding of what this means in Jesus' name. Amen.

Day 9: Risen with Christ

"*And hath raised us up together, and made us sit together in heavenly places in Christ Jesus*" (Ephesians 2:6; KJV).

"*If ye then be risen with Christ, seek those things which are above, where Christ sitteth on the right hand of God. ² Set your affection on things above, not on things on the earth*" (Colossians 3:1-2; KJV).

Under the New Covenant, we are risen with Christ Jesus our Lord, and we are to set our affections on things above.

To "set" is a deliberate action. Therefore, we must disregard all distractions and focus on things of eternal value. This will be reflected in our daily choices and the decisions that we make. In other words, we need to partner with Jesus Christ, our Lord, in relating to the things of the Kingdom of God.

Confession: I am risen with Christ Jesus my Lord; therefore, I set my affections on things above and make decisions based on eternal values in Jesus' name. Amen.

Day 10: Intimacy with God

"For this is the covenant that I will make with the house of Israel after those days, says the Lord: I will put My laws in their mind and write them on their hearts; and I will be their God, and they shall be My people. [11] None of them shall teach his neighbor, and none his brother, saying, 'Know the Lord,' for all shall know Me, from the least of them to the greatest of them" (Hebrews 8:10-11).

Knowing God is our covenant, right? We just need to take the necessary steps to get to know God our Father better by knowing His Word, renewing our minds, spending time with the Lord, and seeing ourselves the way the Lord sees us. What good Father does not want to have a close relationship with their son or daughter? How much more God our Father?

What a privilege we have under this New Covenant!

Prayer: Thank you, Father, for making me your child because of the sacrifice of Jesus Christ. Father, I ask for the grace to know you better as I ought to in Jesus' name. Amen.

DAY 11: THE INNER WITNESS

"*The Spirit Himself bears witness with our spirit that we are children of God*" (Romans 8:16).

What a privilege and honour to have the witness in our spirits that we are children of God! The Old Testament saints did not have that, as Jesus Christ, our Lord, had not yet paid the price for us to become children of God.

The Holy Spirit that bears witness to our sonship also bears witness to other things. So, as we go about our day, let us be aware of the inner witness regarding when to move, stop, speak, and when not to speak, and so on.

The Holy Spirit is the spirit of truth, and He will always guide us into all truth. We just need to learn the ways of the Spirit.

Prayer: Lord, help me to be sensitive to your promptings and leadings, in Jesus' name. Amen.

Day 12: We Are Healed

"*Who his own self bare our sins in his own body on the tree, that we, being dead to sins, should live unto righteousness: by whose stripes ye were healed*" (1 Peter 2:24; KJV).

Jesus bore stripes, and we are already healed. In the Book of Isaiah, we have more insight into what will occur on the cross (Isaiah 53:3-5). We walk by faith and appropriate what belongs to us by faith. The just shall live by faith (Hebrews 10:38). This spiritual reality must be assessed by faith.

Walking in health is part of our covenant.

Prayer: Lord, you bore my sicknesses and pains so that I don't have to bear them. I asked for spiritual understanding to help me access what already belongs to me through the sacrifice of Jesus in Jesus' name. Amen.

Day 13: We Have Obtained the Mercy of God

"*Which in time past were not a people, but are now the people of God: which had not obtained mercy, but now have obtained mercy*" (1 Peter 2:10; KJV).

We have now obtained the mercy of God. By His mercy, we are the people of God. Therefore, we need to see ourselves as objects of God's mercy. Our own works have not saved us.

This is why the Scripture tells us:

"But sanctify the Lord God in your hearts: and be ready always to give an answer to every man that asketh you a reason of the hope that is in you with meekness and fear" (1 Peter 3:15; KJV).

As we go about our days, let us extend God's mercy to others by sharing Christ with them.

Prayer: Father God, I thank you for the mercy that I have obtained through knowing Jesus Christ as Lord and Saviour. Help me, Lord, to be a true representation of your mercy to others in Jesus' name. Amen.

DAY 14: ACCESS TO THE MERCY OF GOD

"*Seeing then that we have a great High Priest who has passed through the heavens, Jesus the Son of God, let us hold fast our confession. ¹⁵ For we do not have a High Priest who cannot sympathize with our weaknesses, but was in all points tempted as we are, yet without sin.* **¹⁶ Let us therefore come boldly to the throne of grace, that we may obtain mercy and find grace to help in time of need**" (Hebrews 4:14-16).

According to the above scripture, we need to come to the throne of grace to obtain mercy in time of need.

We all need the mercy of God. Have you done something wrong and regretted it? Then, simply repent and ask for God's mercy. God is well able to fix the problem. And to make matters even better, the Lord asks us to come and obtain mercy.

In other words, God wants to bestow His mercy on us. He only wants us to ask.

Prayer: Make your prayer specific and ask for the mercy of God in that situation.

Day 15: Access to the Grace of God

"*Let us therefore come boldly to the throne of grace, that we may obtain mercy and find grace to help in time of need*" (Hebrews 4:16).

Have you run out of your own ability? There is grace available for us all. We just have to come boldly and ask for it. Grace enables us to do what we cannot do in our own strength and ability.

Paul gives us more insight regarding what the grace of God can do for us: "*But by the grace of God I am what I am, and His grace toward me was not in vain; but I labored more abundantly than they all, yet not I, but the grace of God which was with me*" (1 Corinthians 15:10).

Paul clearly states here that God's grace helped him labour more abundantly than others. Do you need help today? Then ask for grace.

Prayer: Be specific about what you need grace for and ask the Lord for it.

DAY 16: WE HAVE BEEN GIVEN THE MINISTRY OF RECONCILIATION

"*Therefore, if anyone is in Christ, he is a new creation; old things have passed away; behold, all things have become new. ¹⁸ Now all things are of God, who has reconciled us to Himself through Jesus Christ, and has given us the ministry of reconciliation, ¹⁹ that is, that God was in Christ reconciling the world to Himself, not [d]imputing their trespasses to them, and has committed to us the word of reconciliation*" (2 Corinthians 5:17-19).

From this scripture, we can see that Jesus Christ, our Lord, has reconciled us to God and given us the ministry of reconciliation.

We are to go out and tell others that God is not holding their sins against them, but He would have all to be saved and come unto the knowledge of Christ (1 Timothy 2:4). The price has been paid. We are to announce to the world that all they need to do is receive the sacrifice and finished work of Christ by making Jesus Christ the Lord and Saviour of their lives. Jesus Christ has become a sin for us all. We just need to receive it.

The Lord relies on us to share the good news (Mark 16:15-16).

We are ambassadors for Christ (2 Corinthians 5:20).

Prayer: Lord, as I go about my day today, give me sensitivity to know with whom I need to share the good news of the gospel in Jesus' name. Amen.

Day 17: We Are the Righteousness of God in Christ

"*For he hath made him to be sin for us, who knew no sin; that we might be made the righteousness of God in him*" (2 Corinthians 5:21; KJV).

Just think about that. Jesus Christ, our Lord, knew no sin, yet He was made sin for us. This is how much the Lord loves us, as we can have right standing with Him. Our righteousness is not in ourselves but in Christ Jesus, our Lord.

Have you ever felt otherwise? There is good news: we are the righteousness of God in Christ Jesus. When we sin, we simply repent and ask the Lord to forgive us. Not only will He forgive us, but He will also cleanse us from all unrighteousness (1 John 1:9).

The Bible says the righteous are as bold as lions (Proverbs 28:1).

Confession: Thank you, Lord, that I am now the righteousness of God in Christ Jesus. I can come boldly unto the throne of grace because of what Jesus Christ has done for us.

Day 18: Jesus Christ is Our High Priest

"*For we do not have a High Priest who cannot sympathize with our weaknesses, but was in all points tempted as we are, yet without sin*" (Hebrews 4:15).

In the Old Covenant, priests carried out sacrifices on behalf of the people. Every year, the priests had to sacrifice to put away sin (Hebrews 9:25), but Jesus Christ, our High Priest, has put away sin by the sacrifice of Himself (Hebrews 9:26), and this has been done once and for all (Hebrews 10:10).

Jesus Christ is our High Priest forever (Hebrews 7:17).

Sin has been dealt with. Jesus Christ is our High Priest. When we sin, we repent and ask God to forgive us in Jesus' name. Jesus Christ is forever our High Priest.

Prayer: Father, I thank you that Jesus Christ is my high priest forever.

Day 19: A New Creation in Christ Jesus

"*Therefore, if anyone is in Christ, he is a new creation; old things have passed away; behold, all things have become new*" (2 Corinthians 5:17).

The Old Testament saints, despite learning so much from them, were not new creations in Christ Jesus. This only became available after the sacrifice of Jesus Christ our Lord.

It does not matter what we have done in the past. If anyone is in Christ, he is a new creation. Our spirits are reborn by the power of the Holy Spirit when we give our lives to Christ. This is the mercy of God. New means new, brand new.

"*Therefore if anyone is in Christ [that is, grafted in, joined to Him by faith in Him as Savior], he is a new creature [reborn and renewed by the Holy Spirit]; the old things [the previous moral and spiritual condition] have passed away. Behold, new things have come [because spiritual awakening brings a new life]*" (2 Corinthians 5:17; AMP).

What a privilege we have in Christ!

This invitation is open to all. If you don't have Christ yet, the price has already been paid. You just need to say yes. For "whoever calls on the name of the Lord shall be saved" (Romans 10:13).

Confession: Father, I thank you for what Jesus Christ did for me, and I am now a new creation in Christ Jesus.

Day 20: Dead to Sin

"*Who his own self bare our sins in his own body on the tree, that we, being dead to sins, should live unto righteousness: by whose stripes ye were healed*" (1 Peter 2:24; KJV).

According to this scripture, we are dead to sin. The Old Testament saints were not dead to sin, yet they had to live upright. This was one reason the priests then had to make an atonement for sins annually (Hebrews 10:3). Jesus Christ offered one sacrifice for sins (Hebrews 10:12), and Jesus Christ bore our sins in His own body (1 Peter 2:24). Hence, we are dead to sin.

The Bible further tells us that sin shall not have dominion over us (Romans 6:14).

Are you struggling with your flesh? Did you know that you have dominion over it? We just need to acknowledge who we are in the spirit and walk in the Spirit (Galatians 5:16). The key to victory is walking in the Spirit. In other words, focus on and act like who Scripture says you are.

Ask the Lord to help you. Ask for grace and further understanding of what it means to walk in the Spirit. The good news is that we are dead to sin, and we are to yield ourselves unto God.

Prayer: Father, I thank you, and I will bring glory to your name by walking in the Spirit and acknowledging who I now am in Christ. Thank you for your grace in Jesus' name. Amen.

DAY 21: ABILITY TO BEAR FRUIT OF THE SPIRIT

"*But the fruit of the Spirit is love, joy, peace, longsuffering, kindness, goodness, faithfulness, 23 [g]gentleness, self-control. Against such there is no law. 24 And those who are Christ's have crucified the flesh with its passions and desires. 25 If we live in the Spirit, let us also walk in the Spirit*" (Galatians 5:22-25).

As we grow in the Lord, the fruit of the Spirit will manifest in our lives. As we look back, we should see an increase in patience, kindness, and faithfulness (keeping our word and our commitments). All this is part of the fruit of the Spirit. The Holy Spirit now lives in us, and as we grow and yield more to Him, His fruit will be evident in our lives.

Confession: As I grow in the Lord, the fruit of the Spirit will be more and more evident in my life, bringing glory to the Father in Jesus' name. Amen.

Day 22: We Can Call God Our Father

"*For you did not receive the spirit of bondage again to fear, but you received the Spirit of adoption by whom we cry out, "Abba,[e] Father, The Spirit Himself bears witness with our spirit that we are children of God*," (Romans 8:15-16).

We can call God our Father. This is because the God and Father of our Lord Jesus Christ is also our own Father.

Have you had an experience with a good earthly father? If you have, then be rest assured that God our Father cannot be compared with even the best of the earthly fathers.

Seeing God as our Father will deepen our fellowship with the Lord.

"That which we have seen and heard we declare to you, that you also may have fellowship with us; and truly our fellowship is with the Father and with His Son Jesus Christ" (1 John 1:3).

When the disciples asked Jesus Christ to teach them to pray, the first sentence was, "Our Father in heaven" (Matthew 6:9).

As we begin to meditate and have a deeper understanding of our Heavenly Father, it will greatly impact our walk with the Lord.

Prayer: Father God, l ask that you give me a greater revelation so that l may know you better as Father in Jesus' name. Amen.

Day 23: Justified By Faith

Therefore, having been justified by faith, [a] we have peace with God through our Lord Jesus Christ (Romans 5:1).

Under the New Covenant, we are justified by faith. Faith in what Jesus Christ has done for us and not by works.

We must be careful to keep our focus on what Christ has already done for us. We are simply beneficiaries of all that Christ has done for us. We just have to grow up in the knowledge of what already belongs to us. We have been saved by grace through faith (Ephesians 2:8-9).

We must be grateful for what Jesus Christ our Lord has made available to us.

Prayer: Father, I thank you for what you have made available to me through Jesus Christ our Lord, in Jesus' name. I now walk by faith and not by sight.

DAY 24: FORGIVENESS OF SINS

"In Him we have redemption through His blood, the forgiveness of sins, according to the riches of His grace" (Ephesians 1:7).

Forgiveness of sins is part of the New Covenant. We have been forgiven our sins, not according to what we have done but according to the riches of His grace.

The scriptures further tell us that God will no longer remember our sins (Hebrews 8:12). Once we ask the Lord to forgive us of any sin, He will forgive us. This is part of our New Covenant.

We don't need to go to anyone and ask them to pray for us. Instead, we approach the Lord ourselves and ask Him to forgive us.

Once we repent and confess our sins, we know that the Lord has forgiven us, and we must forgive ourselves.

Not only does the Lord forgive us of our sins, but He also cleanses us from all unrighteousness (1 John 1:9).

Confession: Father, thank you that Jesus Christ's death on the cross made it possible for sins to be forgiven. I no longer need to live in sin consciousness, but in the knowledge that I am now the righteousness of God in Christ.

DAY 25: PEACE WITH GOD

"*Therefore, having been justified by faith, [a]we have peace with God through our Lord Jesus Christ*" (Romans 5:1).

In the world, people go to many lengths sometimes to be at peace with someone. When you are at peace with someone, you can approach them whenever necessary.

How much more God our Father? We have peace with God through Jesus Christ our Lord and can now approach God our Father boldly. The Lord is waiting for us to draw near unto Him (James 4:8).

Confession: Father, I thank you that I now have peace with you. Jesus Christ is my peace.

Day 26: God's Love Has Been Poured into Our Hearts

Now hope does not disappoint, because the love of God has been poured out in our hearts by the Holy Spirit who was given to us (Romans 5:5).

We can walk in love and love God because we have already been given what it takes. The Holy Spirit has poured the love of God into our hearts.

This is actually an answer to Jesus' prayer before He paid the price for us: *"And I have declared to them Your name, and will declare it, **that the love with which You loved Me may be in them, and I in them*** (John 17:26).

As we go about our day and encounter difficult situations, we just need to yield to the love of God already in our hearts. We will also come across people whom we will have compassion for. This is God's love in our hearts.

Prayer: Father, I thank you that your love has been poured out into my heart. By your help and grace, I will yield to that love as I go about my day and be a blessing to others in Jesus' name. Amen.

Day 27: We Can Be Led by the Spirit of God

"For as many as are led by the Spirit of God, these are sons of God" (Romans 8:14).

Now that we are sons of God, we can be led by the Spirit of God. Therefore, we need to learn how to yield to the leading of the Spirit of God.

Under the Old Covenant, the people had to go to prophets to find out the direction of the Lord. In the New Covenant, we are led by the Spirit of God.

To be led by the Spirit of God, we must let the word of Christ dwell richly in us, meditate on the Word of God, pray in the Spirit, wait on the Lord, ask the Lord for direction, and listen to our spirits.

Prayer: Lord, help me to be more sensitive to your leading by your Spirit, in Jesus' name.

Day 28: Living Through Christ Jesus

"*In this the love of God was manifested toward us, that God has sent His only begotten Son into the world, that we might live through Him*" (1 John 4:9).

This perspective is so important as a Christian. Looking at this scripture, one reason Jesus Christ came was so that we could "live through Him".

We don't need to live this Christian walk in our own strength. Instead, we are called to live "through Him".

This is a privilege under our better covenant.

Are you struggling in any area? Ask the Lord for help, and yield to His help as we live through Him.

Confession: Thank you, Father, that I can now live my life through Christ Jesus, my ever-present help.

Day 29: Seated With Christ in Heavenly Places

"*And raised us up together, and made us sit together in the heavenly places in Christ Jesus*" (Ephesians 2:6).

This is our position of authority in Christ Jesus. We must see ourselves there, especially in the place of prayer and in exercising our authority.

It is all about what Jesus Christ has done for us. When God raised Christ Jesus from the dead, He raised us all up together. A revelation of this will take our prayer life to another level.

We need to meditate on this truth so it becomes a place of reality in our prayer life.

Prayer: Father, thank you for the authority you gave me in Christ Jesus under this New Covenant.

Day 30: Authority to Use the Name of Jesus

"And these signs will follow those who [d]believe: In My name they will cast out demons; they will speak with new tongues; 18 they[e] will take up serpents; and if they drink anything deadly, it will by no means hurt them; they will lay hands on the sick, and they will recover" (Mark 16:17-18).

We have been given the authority to use the name of Jesus Christ. From the above verse, all these signs follow those who believe, and all will be done in the name of Jesus Christ. Everything that Jesus Christ, our Lord, accomplished for us is backed up by that name. We are not doing anything in our own name but in the name of our Lord and Saviour, Jesus Christ.

Peter and John knew what they had, and so should we.

Then Peter said, "Silver and gold I do not have, but what I do have I give you: In the name of Jesus Christ of Nazareth, rise up and walk (Acts 3:6).

As we go about our day, let us remember what we have.

Confession: The name of Jesus belongs to me; the power invested in that name belongs to me. Thank you, Father, for what you have given me.

Day 31: The Promise of the Holy Spirit

"*Nevertheless I tell you the truth. It is to your advantage that I go away; for if I do not go away, the Helper will not come to you; but if I depart, I will send Him to you*" (John 16:7).

Jesus Christ promised us the Holy Spirit when He finished His work on earth and went to the Father. The Holy Spirit came to earth on Pentecost (Acts 2:1-4). Now, all we need to do is ask for Him as believers in Christ (Luke 11:13).

The Holy Spirit has a great role to play in the life of every believer. He guides us into all truth and He shows us things to come (John 16:13). He teaches and brings things to our memory (John 14:26). He empowers (Acts 1:8) and helps us to abound in hope (Romans 15:13). The list goes on.

We have the person of the godhead abiding with us forever (John 14:16).

Prayer: Thank you, Father, for the person of the Holy Spirit you gave to me. Lord, I ask for the grace to know Him better in Jesus' name. Amen.

DAY 32: THE GIFTS OF THE HOLY SPIRIT CAN WORK THROUGH US

"There are [d]diversities of gifts, but the same Spirit. **5** There are differences of ministries, but the same Lord. **6** And there are diversities of activities, but it is the same God who works [e]all in all. **7** But the manifestation of the Spirit is given to each one for the profit of all: **8** for to one is given the word of wisdom through the Spirit, to another the word of knowledge through the same Spirit, **9** to another faith by the same Spirit, to another gifts of healings by [f]the same Spirit, **10** to another the working of miracles, to another prophecy, to another discerning of spirits, to another different kinds of tongues, to another the interpretation of tongues. **11** But one and the same Spirit works all these things, distributing to each one individually as He wills" (1 Corinthians 12:4-11).

Have you ever attended a conference or church meeting where the gifts of the Spirit were in operation? This is part of our inheritance. The gifts of the Spirit can manifest through any believer who learn how to yield to the Holy Spirit.

At work and in our everyday life, the gifts of the Spirit can flow through us as long as we have learnt to yield and obey.

Imagine having a word of knowledge for one of your work colleagues or someone you meet at the store. This is part of the role of the Holy Spirit. He has gifts, which we can all partake of.

Prayer: Father, l pray and thank you for the precious Holy Spirit and His gifts. Make me a vessel that He can freely flow through and bless those around me in Jesus' name. Amen.

Day 33: Prosperity

"*For you know the grace of our Lord Jesus Christ, that though He was rich, yet for your sakes He became poor, that you through His poverty might become rich*" (2 Corinthians 8:9).

"*Beloved, I wish above all things that thou mayest prosper and be in health, even as thy soul prospereth*" (3 John 3:2; KJV).

The Lord wants us to prosper, and prosperity is not limited to money. The Lord is not against us having money. It is the love of money that is the root of all evil (1 Timothy 6:10).

The Bible also talks about our soul prospering. A prosperous soul is a soul that the word of God has renewed.

It takes money to preach the gospel and reach the lost. It takes money to advance the kingdom of God and to be a blessing to others.

BISI OLADIPUPO

Confession: Thank you, Father, that Jesus Christ became poor so that through His poverty, I might be rich. I take hold of this in Jesus' name. Amen.

Day 34: Christ Now Lives in Us

"*I have been crucified with Christ; it is no longer I who live, but Christ lives in me; and the life which I now live in the flesh I live by faith in the Son of God, who loved me and gave Himself for me*" (Galatians 2:20).

Under our better covenant, Christ lives in us. Just as Jesus Christ, during His earthly ministry, said that the "Father that is in me is doing the works" (John 14:10), so can we say that Christ in us is doing the works. We must also remember that Christ in us is the hope of glory (Colossians 1:27).

When we walk in the consciousness of this spiritual reality, we will find it easy to cast all our cares upon the Lord and know that the life we live in the flesh, we live with His ability. We will also find it easier to minister to others.

BISI OLADIPUPO

Confession: Christ lives in me; therefore, I am not living my life in the flesh in my strength.

Day 35: Boldness to Come unto the Throne of Grace

"For we do not have a High Priest who cannot sympathize with our weaknesses, but was in all *points* tempted as *we are, yet* without sin. ¹⁶ Let us therefore come boldly to the throne of grace, that we may obtain mercy and find grace to help in time of need" (Hebrews 4:15-16).

When we pray, we need to visualise ourselves approaching a throne. This throne is called the throne of grace. God, our Father, sits on His throne (Psalms 45:6), and grace is available at that throne. What makes it even better is that we can come boldly because of what Jesus Christ has done for us.

In times of struggle and need, mercy and grace are available when we ask. What a great privilege we have!

Action: Take any struggle to the throne of grace. Ask for grace and mercy.

DAY 36: WE ARE THE TEMPLE OF THE LIVING GOD

"*Do you not know that you are the temple of God and that the Spirit of God dwells in you?*" (1 Corinthians 3:16).

Just imagine God the Father living in us. We are the temple of the living God.

In the natural world, temples are taken care of, especially if they host important things. However, we are more valuable than any earthly temple you can see on earth because we are the temple of the living God. Therefore, we do have to take care of our bodies. This has two sides: what we eat and how we treat our bodies.

"*18 Flee sexual immorality. Every sin that a man does is outside the body, but he who commits sexual immorality sins against his own body. 19 Or do you not know that your body is the temple of the Holy Spirit who is in you, whom you have from God, and you are not your own? 20 For you were bought at a price; therefore glorify God in your body [g] and in your spirit, which are God's"* (1 Corinthians 6:18-20).

Prayer: Lord, thank you that the Holy Spirit now lives in me and that my body is your temple. This temple will bring glory to you in Jesus' name. Amen.

Day 37: The Kingdom of God is Within You

Now when He was asked by the Pharisees when the kingdom of God would come, He answered them and said, "The kingdom of God does not come with observation; ²¹ nor will they say, [f]'See here!' or 'See there!' For indeed, the kingdom of God is [g]within you" (John 17:20–21).

The Bible tells us that the kingdom of God is righteousness, peace, and joy in the Holy Spirit (John 14:17).

Because Christ lives in us, we can release peace wherever we go. We can pray for others and manifest the kingdom of God to them. When we pray for the sick and people's needs, we release the kingdom of God.

As we go about, we must walk in the consciousness that we are kingdom carriers.

Prayer: Lord, as I go about my day, I pray that I will be sensitive to those you would want me to release your kingdom to in Jesus' name. Amen.

DAY 38: DEMONSTRATION OF THE POWER OF GOD

"For the kingdom of God is not in word, but in power" (1 Corinthians 4:20).

Have you ever experienced the power of God in a service? Did you know that this can be an everyday occurrence in our lives?

Just imagine sharing the gospel with someone who is arguing with you. You suddenly have a word of knowledge about pain in their body that they never discussed with you. They allow you to pray for them; you do, and they are healed.

The person just experienced the power of God. We can manifest the power of God with the help of the Holy Spirit, and this will go far beyond our convincing words.

Prayer: Lord, I ask for boldness to demonstrate your power today as I go about my day in Jesus' name. Amen.

DAY 39: ABILITY TO PRAY IN THE HOLY SPIRIT

But you, beloved, building yourselves up on your most holy faith, praying in the Holy Spirit (Jude 1:20).

And these signs will follow those who [d]believe: In My name they will cast out demons; they will speak with new tongues (Mark 16:17).

We have no record that the Old Testament saints could speak in tongues, yet, Paul said, *"I speak with tongues more that you all"* (1 Corinthians 14:18). The Old Testament saints had amazing answers to prayers prayed in their natural language. We have the privilege of our spirit speaking to God and speaking mysteries in the spirit (1 Corinthians 14:2), as well as praying in our understanding.

If the Old Testament saints praying in their understanding had outstanding results, including it not raining for three years (James 5:17), how much more can we do with the help of the Holy Spirit speaking mysteries?

There are so many benefits to praying in the Spirit. Let us lay hold of this great privilege given to us.

Confession: Father, thank you for the privilege of praying in the Spirit under this better covenant.

Day 40: Ability to Live for Christ

> *"For the love of Christ compels us, because we judge thus: that if One died for all, then all died;* **15** *and He died for all, that those who live should live no longer for themselves, but for Him who died for them and rose again* (2 Corinthians 5:14-15).

We are to live for Christ now.

In the Old Covenant, we have saints who walked with God and loved God. Under the New Covenant, we can do much better. God's love has been poured into our hearts (Romans 5:5). We are to live for Christ and love God (1 John 4:19). We are not to pursue our own agenda but God's plan for our lives.

The rewards of living for Christ and leaving behind our own agenda have rewards both in this life and in the life to come.

Let this be our hearts' cry: *"For to me, to live is Christ"* (Philippians 1:21).

Prayer: Thank you, Father, for the sacrifice of Jesus Christ. I will give my life fully and totally for you in Jesus' name.

SALVATION PRAYER

Father God, I come to you in Jesus' name. I admit that I am a sinner, and I now receive the sacrifice that Jesus Christ paid for me.

I confess with my mouth the Lord Jesus, and I believe in my heart that God raised Him from the dead.

I now declare that Jesus Christ is my Lord and Saviour.

Thank you, Father, for saving me in Jesus' name.

I am now your child. Amen.

If you've said this prayer for the first time, send an email to Bisiwriter@gmail.com . Start reading your Bible and ask the Lord to guide you to a good church.

Also By Bisi

1. The Twelve Apostles of Jesus Christ: Lessons We Can Learn

2. The Lord's Cup in Communion: The Significance of taking the Lord's Supper

3. Different Ways to Receive Healing from Scripture and Walk in Health

4. Believing on The Name of Jesus Christ: What Every Believer Needs to Know

5. The Mind and Your Christian Walk: The Impact of the mind on our Christian walk

6. Relationship Skills in the Bible: Scriptural Principles of relating to others

7. The Nature of God's Kingdom: The Characteristics of the Kingdom of God

8. The Person of the Holy Spirit

9. 41 Insights from the Book of Revelation

10. The Importance of Spiritual Discernment

11. God Speaks Through Nature

12. It's All About the Heart

13. A Better Covenant: A Look at the Covenants of God and Our Better Covenant

About Author

Bisi Oladipupo has been a Christian for many years and lives in the United Kingdom with her family.

She has attended a few Bible colleges and obtained a diploma in Biblical Studies from the UK. She also has an associate degree in Bible and Theology from a USA Bible college.

She is a teacher of God's Word and coordinates Bible studies.

Her author page is www.bisiwriter.com

She writes regularly, and her blog website is www.inspiredwords.org

You can contact Bisi by email at bisiwriter@gmail.com

Afterword

If you enjoyed this book, please take a few moments to write a review of it online at the store where it was purchased. Thank you!

www.ingramcontent.com/pod-product-compliance
Lightning Source LLC
Chambersburg PA
CBHW030043100526
44590CB00011B/316